Request Line at Noon

Poems

Lee Jangwook

Translation by
Sun Kim and Tsering Wangmo

A Forsythia Book

CODHILL

Codhill Press
New Paltz, New York

CODHILL

THIS IS A CODHILL BOOK

Codhill books are published by David Appelbaum for Codhill Press

ISBN 1-930337-87-6
First Edition

This publication was made possible in part by the generous support of the Literature Translation Institute of Korea (LTI Korea).

Book Design by Alicia Fox
Cover art © Alicia Fox
www.aliciafoxdesign.com

Library of Congress Cataloging-in-Publication Data

Names: Yi, Chang-uk, 1968- author. | Kim, S on-gy ong (Literary translator), translator.
Title: Request line at noon : poems / Lee Jangwook ; translation by Sunkyoung Kim.
Description: First Edition | New Paltz, New York : Codhill Press, 2016 | Includes bibliographical references and index.
Identifiers: LCCN 2015043095 | ISBN 1930337876 (alk. paper)
Subjects: LCSH: Yi, Chang-uk, 1968—Translations into English.
Classification: LCC PL994.9.C437 A2 2016 | DDC 895.71/5—dc23
LC record available at http://lccn.loc.gov/2015043095

Request Line at Noon

Contents

Request Line at Noon

Wires

We are connected firmly
We are linked

From the top of a utility pole, a wire mechanic
Transmits a signal somewhere

We set our empty gaze skyward
Like clouds caught in an air current at 8000 meters

I want to dismiss you
I miss you

A resident bird on the wire
Looks ahead until
Something vital pierces through it

From Many Worlds

We had our own lovers
Spent our own autumn
Thought of our own Africa
From many worlds

We faced our lonely aging at last
Became poor for no reason at last
Took in our petty fate at last

We came together from many worlds
When he turned back firmly,
She danced by chance in the same rhythm
And off to sea you went in search of forgotten music

At last we became our own dusk
And came back to our own season
If not thinking about anything, all would turn into water, so
He paused in a zero point position
And she began praying hard
You might just look back

The hot summer will be over by Christmas
We came together from many worlds
And we were still in love
Lonely, sweet and lasting love

Infighter

Mr. Elephant's Postcard

Look at the relieved people's faces, over there.
But if faraway clouds declare a war
I shall fight like a mute after all.
Duk-koo Kim's 14th round, remember his last step?
No love, no realism,
Just as right in front of my eyes there is no part of you that is not me.
However, where on earth is *here*, emptying itself out all of a sudden
Like a tip of the twig that missed the apple?
After drinking a shot of *soju*, walking through the falling snow,
I want to reach the most ridiculous winter
From where I can never come back again
And where the cat that disappeared just before my eyes has arrived.
In a big boxing robe
I will march into the square ring.
Don't cry for me, Argentina.
You have never imagined the sea I was staring at, have you?
So please forget me some mornings.
We only become weak when recalling people.
As I looked out of the window vacantly like a fallen apple,
Over there, slowly to the western sea, a bird flew away.
When I was wavering stolidly in the vague light,
The clouds' countenances, knew everything.
But let us not look back, otherwise, we will harden like stone,
And can never again deliver a counterpunch.
Farewell. Don't cry for me.
There is no proof that there was a cat? So,
Render unto Caesar the things that are Caesar's,
And unto clouds the things that are of clouds'.
I am the untiring
Sparring partner of clouds.

Zombie Walking

As the rain started
I became clear
I forgot you
Became expressionless for a moment
Had breakfast
And slept

I walked endless streets by day
Friends either aggressive or pessimistic
My body hardened

I murdered one person
And loved two
And wept for a moment
Then listened to some music

My love remained unchanged
My death remained unchanged

I am an ascetic
And have future ambitions

When 1968 came
The Prague Spring came to an end
Led Zeppelin was formed
Su-yeong Kim died

Ever afterwards for a long time
I wasn't born yet,
As the rain started
I simply wept for a moment
And proceeded

Decision

When I wake up in the morning everything will stop.
Little pebbles will quieten coldly.
Things will retreat.

I cancel an appointment. I put off
Washing my face, preparing a meal, going to work.
Windows freeze up.
The inside and outside air fiercely
Produces solid water drops. Gradually,
Everything comes to an end.
A glass is metal somewhere remote,
On the giddy horizon a strange mind blows in.

I want to call my friends.
However, I shouldn't regret too many things.
A mysterious past is what I don't have,
An elderly father is what I have,
I am only here now.

A frightening thought flashes in my mind.
Only one thought
Binds me.
I am frozen. Instantly
The moment of five minutes ago and the distant future reach me.
Slowly, I raise myself.

How Odd

Someone suddenly becomes amused
And someone suddenly gets exhausted
As tomorrow comes,
Someone disappears out of my life all of a sudden

In the morning ulterior motives went away
I moved forward with the power of positivity
Thank gravity, for without it
Where would the past decade go?
And again where would yesterday be?

I became indifferent like a penguin
No leaflets in back streets
And I couldn't imagine satellite altitudes
Yet the night was long in the Arctic

Oddly we paid
Our pension fee regularly
The future broke out
We still believed in love

Over there, waddling
The penguin approached
It looked as if thinking of something
A penguin no less,
How odd

Perfect Night

Tonight goes only from nine to eleven
Nine to eleven, this night

A woman who jumped off the 8th floor of Jugong apartment
Lay on the railing of the second floor
Her long hair dangling
There is no music tonight

From nine to eleven, sitting
In front of a big fish tank at a teahouse near the station,
I stroke her long hair
I think of strange times,
The tropical fish under the fluorescent light
Sway without remorse

And the long-haired woman
Doesn't think of tonight; nine to eleven,
Falling asleep, listening to the sound of dehydrating mandarin peels
She's not swaying in her dream

Tonight goes only from nine to eleven
As tonight is only night from nine to eleven

Happy New Year

Mr. Elephant's postcard

To you, I am a rumor.
I don't disappear.
I am flexible like a plastic bag
Floating away in the sky of Jongno.
Cars pass through the landing point.
As my weight
Gets closer to zero,
I recalled you eagerly
All night long holding my head up.
Speed itself is nothing.
There is only distance between things.
I can stop any time.
I want to be showered with perfect retro spirits
Like the classical hatred for the bourgeois.
The low-pressure trough's moving path
That rules me or,
The laughter of a home drama at eight p.m.
I will be merry.
In the sky of Kyobo Book Centre
A plastic bag in a pause,
Infinite probabilities penetrate its surface.
Let us not be eloquent.
I love you.

Imbalanced Thought

The objects move inch by inch inside,
The armchair now in a slightly different position,
Lying down on my side on the couch,
I think of things that the armchair hid when it moved:
The table clock,
Rosa Luxemburg's last moment,
Or the post-it on the refrigerator,
Now I see the room has become slightly slanted
It was a different arrangement
Three minutes ago,
Three years ago

It seems like someone had a meal and left;
A friend deep in thought,
My mother from a long time ago,
Or the unseen herbivore,
But the curve outside the window drawn by pigeons,
Where did it disappear?

Like clouds meeting one's gaze by chance,
The room, slanted a little as if pouring out somewhere
I am suffering from persistent doubts
As I'm made of chance
Now a man crosses next year's crosswalk
With a different look

The herbivore,
Standing by the unlit signboard of the Samsung Service Center,
Stares vacantly at his back
This passing dawn along with
The trembling long horn
I drop my head a little,
Adjusting to the angle of the sunlight's rays
As though just now my thoughts are
Pouring out somewhere

Request Line at Noon

We were friendly,
Inconsiderate.
Everyone moved forward to an end.
You lost your love
And I skipped rope.
The surging music
At the minimum altitude of my soul;
The music from the "Request Line At Noon"
We were always
Flowing away regularly.
While someone spent their last moments on this earth
The cynical made the world go round.
A kiss scene from a movie theater's sign
Hung on the street
And autumn readily deepened.
I lost my love
And you skipped rope,
The music from the "Request Line At Noon."
For the cynical,
Till the end,
We flew around the sky at noon.

The Nineteenth Century's Rain

When the nineteenth century's rain comes,
I will call you on Thursday.
Thursday,
I will call you on the sole Thursday.
I lost interest in martyrs today
And kept shaking my head.
Since yesterday everything is asymmetry.
I want to meet a woman from the Middle Ages;
Refreshing everything, once again, as going around corners in alleys,
Knowing that kind of witchcraft.
For love and sunlight's sake, please,
Allow euthanasia
To keep that endless music from playing all of a sudden
While walking night streets.
Like a simple insect, I am transforming
And wandering in search of lost raindrops.
Calling a heartless woman
Who loves a circle so,
She has already become the circle.
I am a skill-less magician,
If I go around the corners,
Thursday will show up like magic.
I don't like martyrs,
The martyrs from the Nine O'clock News,
So I shall call in the rain.
Sweet Thursday,
Again on the sole Thursday,
If the nineteenth century's rain comes.

Giraffe's Love

The mourner's house was obvious.
Everything was settled.
After taking off their black leather shoes,
Uncertain people kept sitting down.
Though living at the same time as giraffes,
The one who didn't think of giraffes,
The one who has kept piling on tomorrow's nightmares,
And the one who had dashed out the world five minutes ago,
All had a drink.
Hard-boiled midnight hospital
Your five minutes ago,
My smile and
The faraway giraffe's love,
Drew a rapturous curve.
The national security law in effect,
And the falling snow,
All silhouettes did their best
To be spontaneous.
As a late-night taxi accelerated on the Dongbu expressway
A giraffe
Crossed the street
Swaying its long neck.
The giraffe looked back for a moment.
I remember his indifferent eyes,
Forever.

Noises

Eleven a.m. I absorbed the sounds.
Eleven a.m. I was as noisy as possible.
Opening the window I became countless voices,
Transformed into the speed of sound.
As I came inside of you,
I turned into a thirty-seconds memory.
Mother in the rain,
I ran through her rotten body.
I became an infinite form
That rumors scatter around.
I became a carnivore's dirty appetite.
The splendid angles of blood
Running through the blood vessels,
The speed of growing children,
The sound of rotting milk,
I turned into the mouth that
The hero in the silent film opened the widest.
Eleven a.m. I blocked my ears.
Eleven a.m. I closed my eyes.
I fell into perfect silence.

Let Us Meet in Autumn

Today I tottered around like a doll
At Gwanghwamun my joints revolved gently
At Jongno I didn't blink my eyes
Everybody excused my perfection
When my well-built life began
I was endlessly pure
How nice being naked
How nice being very beautiful too
I can forget other people's private lives soon
I have no bias
On the verge of trickling out some words
I can quietly stop
Though I changed my clothes for love
Hyehwa-dong's autumn passed away routinely
And my thoughts were bent like plastic
After turning left at the intersection, facing a convenience store
I stopped and waited for you
Feeling your smile at last
I advanced
Towards you
Step by step

In a Snowy Village

It snowed
He kept his eyeballs in a dry spot
She cut her ears and put them in the bank
I packed the pounding heart in a document envelope
Like bullets waiting to be shot
Children's small teeth sparkled fearfully
As our fingernails and toenails grew lavishly
And fell into the silence of a forest
A cow cried from a distance
Girls wearing *ao dai*
Bachelors flying around
I could neither think
Nor love
Even if the days of the Great Depression come
I should live on with optimistic dreams
A finger and a finger
Touched each other by chance in the sky
Then beautifully it started to snow again
And from the air
Faded away

A Precise Question

Again and again, everything looks different
You were already born
You fell in love
You are traveling last autumn
You smiled flashing on something long forgotten

Today again and again, everything looks different
Your Monday is quiet
And when you close your eyes, outside the window
Jubilant pounding elephants
Stream away like notes

Your hobby is different from yesterday's
And your raining western sea different from the day before yesterday
Your morning is mysterious
Your faith,
Your weekend drama,
And your lonely sleep,

It all looks different
But I will only cast a precise question
At you
With a look as if I have just finished a meal

Ways of Greeting in Africa

The stairs calmly
Showed an image of gravity

We kept moving towards a higher point
And towards a lower point
There was no rhythm to it

The subway map got more complicated that winter
And unwittingly we spent more and more time underground

But every day the newspapers needed black and bold headlines
And we became alone,
Gazed at the passing Sunday afar
From the rooftop where white laundry swung

So, then, let's think about lighter things:
A balloon's love
Rising full speed towards the atmosphere,
A day, too tight-lipped,
And ways of greeting in Africa

I get scared every day like a five-year-old girl and
I love those who can talk about things that I cannot and
I can watch smoke disperse for an hour

When I go up the stairs
And come down the stairs
I see you—
Hello,
In an African way
We greet,
So that our noses meet each other

The Baseball Park Ten Years Later

Today is full of personal relationships.
Today is like baseball ten years later.

You are an unwelcome witness
And my abeyance,
As I bend knees thinking of the third baseman ten years later,
The long autumn, at last, comes to an end.

We are like the thoughts we know, but the thoughts that never
 come up,
Under today's weather, utterly familiar,

We lose ourselves in thoughts of our personal relationships,
In the end, you and I come to understand baseball ten years later.

"Play ball," someone yelled
And I swung the bat with all my strength.
And I ran desperately
To first base, ten years later.

A Note on Summer Impressions in Winter

The city I've never lived in was ablaze
And every day we returned to sleep.
It was fair weather.
There was a dog crouching on the ground
In order to be as void as possible and,
Between the leaves of summer
The snow of December fell.
We grew apart as best we could.
When wearing a thick coat and walking through the haze,

There an old woman passed by the ruins of Baghdad,
Overhead ignited bombers spun,
Yet the children of winter ran around.
As the long waves surged
From beyond the horizon to yesterday's sleep,
We ran eagerly turning our backs to one another.
It was fair weather.
We will meet again in winter
And stick our warm tongues out, like tired dogs.

Travelers

Let's go to Hupo / In Hupo / Let's be the music / Falling down to earth with the simplest look / If we make the horizon from gathering little sways / It's there where old whales drift like the haze / At last, let's go to Hupo

Travel is fun.
Today the ants are marching in a row.
Instinct is fragrant, the hot cicada is dead, and it's summer.

The dot blinks and inches along the navigator. As the summer of me closes my eyes, the winter of you looks on ahead forever. We leave together and come flickering back.

But I feel dizzy.
I've traveled a planet that turns at a frightening speed.
Every day we reach the future, like a cat reduced to jelly
From spinning far too long. You,

My love, where are you?
I'm traveling and my body is erased over and over
Like the flesh of beasts breaking apart in stomachs.
Following the mornings of my dead girl,

Russia, India and Siam, I've traveled through them all.
Will I see romantic revolutionaries if I went to Cuba?
Please take me to the nearest Havana beach.
There I'll sing at the top of my lungs, my hands making a circle.
Cuba is Cuba, Havana is Havana,

But today my hair grows another way.
Have I loved you?
The hair runs long, shedding the boy's look, forgetting the many barbers,
And now toward the last sunset. The hair is glad,
The only creativity as dreams and budding flower beds disappear.

When it rains on me, a strange morning comes to you; when I have no precious things, you blink your eyes in vain; when I read poems as a materialist, you decide at last on one final trip.

Let's all run a lap, a lap around town.
We'll meet. Somewhere we will.

Have you seen this marvelous scene? A moving, winking galaxy vanishing into a black hole? Is that place a vanishing point? All through the night we walked the Cheongpyeong lakeside.

Earthquake

I was thinking of something else.
The condensation on the glass evaporated
As if it had been waiting.
Past the water pipe the glacier began to move.
For a while, a long gone woman remembered me.
I was thinking of something else.
We were passing a moment, uncanny as an alleyway
But the water drained from the rinsed rice subtly quavered.
The photograph on the wall delicately slipped.
The train dove into another thought
Along with the fading background, forever.
When tremors of an unknown epicenter reached out to
Your yesterday and her sleep,
I was thinking of something else.
The trees opened their arms as they achieved silence
And on the thick window of a convenience store
Hot mist descended as if it had been waiting.
Perhaps, all day long
Someone had wanted to talk about life.

Chun-ja

Have you ever been in love?
I raise my head just so like Narcissus.
I get detected by the GPS
And move at a speed that it can't capture.
The earth is spinning with me
At thirty kilometers per second—
I am the standard of disorderly things,
I am a happy, temporary employee.
I love Chun-ja.
Although I hate children and cars
Children and cars ignore me.
Rainy Harbin,
Could it be my last scene?
Even after becoming an android,
I can't take my head off and put it in the fridge.
I love Chun-ja earnestly
So I barely breathe
Sitting by a tree yesterday and today.
Even though I pay my dues to Green Korea United by automatic
   withdrawal
Its newsletters are like an antiseptic room.
Life is flowing away
While I watch satellites in orbit
My expression stays ablaze all day.
However I can swear to you,
I have been in love.
In love with Chun-ja,
In eternal love with Chun-ja.

You and I, as Flowers

You and I bloomed wild like flowers
And grew indifferent like flowers.
You and I, from the road's end to its entrance,
Carried on over and over
Swapping personal pronouns.
We became infinite.

As summer went by, everything was misinformed and,
Since everything was misinformed, the snow fell.
The air was full of unpredictable angles.

"Winter," someone cried out
And everyone understood it.
You and I,
He and I,
Loved the future of flowers;
Audiovisually
Drawn out.

You and him, so dazzling,
The street trees could not look at you
And he and I so swiftly transforming that
Passing birds could not see us.
You and I parted impassively
After talking joyfully.

We devoted ourselves to work or
Made phone calls from a height of fifteen meters.
When I looked out gloomily from the window,
There again you passed by
And flowers bloomed wild behind you.

Out of Orbit

A small screw slowly turns.
On one lengthened rotation,
The wind blows deeper as much as it loosens.
The shelf with a porcelain bowl tips
To fill up the unseen space.
After seeing you off
I took a taxi speeding at one hundred kilometers per hour.
I looked up at the night sky
There were no stars imagining their fall.
The moment a star shifts its orbit
The orchids in the room lower their bloated bodies.
Slumber seeps in like starlight
Into the crevices of your body on the sofa.
However, everything is nothing
But a little transference.
That was what you said while you drank.
Red long lines disappear beyond the four-lane roads.
As I watch myself speeding away with the night sky's gaze upon me
The shelf with the porcelain
Dreams about some sort of fall.
A small screw turns slowly.
To the deeper hole, the wind passes in by degrees.
Beyond the night road
I tilt bit by bit.

Small Talk

In the corridor,
By the vending machine,
On the bus,
I scattered like the jets of a water fountain
Then having dispersed,
I soaked through everything—

With the speed of nails growing,
With the brief moment of silence in between small talks,
With my stare that gazes back while I walk
As if hearing someone call,
With the eyes of a passerby's which the stare meets,
And with the oblivion of the eyes,

A man talks severely on the phone, from the tips of his hair
Into the dark light that grows by degrees
Thrusting up again the tips of his hair,
Along with the mathematic space
Between streaks of rain
Caused by the air from a gust of rain,
From the darkness
That seeps in slowly
Beyond dusk,
At the end of the talks
So short and forgotten
That you and I share,

On the bus,
By the vending machine,
On the sidewalk, at last
I was like the jets of a water fountain

Fire

I'm scared
Every morning I'm amused
So if I round myself off
I will rise inch by inch
I'm scared and
Amused
So will I fake my lines?
Like the sudden roar of an old pro wrestler
I want to play an active role somewhere
Till I love you
Till I grow insidious
In black pants

In the middle of the four-lane roads, Myeong-dong,
In the posture of dreaming love,
In the soul of a hunted witch,
I'll spread my arms
Toward you
And give a wink, taking fate as security
Then the streetlights in the metropolis will go out all at once
And the passersby will freeze
And I will recall the most fateful end
At last I spread out my arms and
Fire, fire, fire
When I open my big mouth
I'm scared
And again amused
Under the eaves of sunset
Coming nearer through the chromatic scale

Phytogenic

As the sunlight unfurls in the shape of a greenhouse,
We grow.
Lifting our chins up
Though we run as fast as we can
Someone, like an illegible foreigner, questions.

Now, where, are, you, all?

I can see that long xylem vessel running through your mouth.
We run hard
And we don't move
Like an old dog summoning a fragrance from afar
Putting its snout in the air.
Flowers occur but you've never
Believed in revolution.
Roots go downward, stems sunward
And then flowers rise in regular succession.

Gravity is infinite.
We are optimists
Growing up in slow motion.
My friends rescue the falling sunlight
Upon all of their bodies.

On my body flowers bloom.
I look long at the air built up around me
By my friends.
I start to reach into the air
Like a beast all alone.
It feels good.

Perhaps the Devil

Perhaps that's it.
In *Roman Holiday* everything is in a retro style
So your face never again comes across my mind.
My thought flashes as if washing out myself.
Today I pay for life insurance
And today is my previous life,
Today everything is irresponsible.
Somehow I feel good.

At last, my memory shrinks like a fresh dead man's.
When I kiss you
You do not know me and
The cars reversing wildly along the Han River.
I finally see the sea for the first time.
The life of a boy, so simple
The first love at the end of the Yushin Regime
Returning from afar,
As I sink beaming into the soft water
Everything is as expected.
Everything is perfect.
As I recede into a single dot
Again everything is perfect.
Perhaps that's it. In *Roman Holiday* the devil,
Perhaps the devil
Flows around in red trousers.
Today, this morning
I too make my way diligently backwards.

Meeting Plaza

We met all the time. When you got close to me your left hand ascended like magic as I raised my right hand to you.
Again and again, we got closer.

We achieved a kind of ground, but why did we get powerless, bit by bit? You didn't think of Orion, I stopped being a man of leisure and we could never escape from each other.

We got together. I would live politely, but you could hate your life in vain.
When I became a silhouette and seized your pupils,
Your worn lips opened, finally.

Farewell.

On my last evening I shall not recall today's greeting. The fox trot music from the Plaza and the military helicopter, *tatata*, flying away,
Life replaces itself in regular succession.

When the plaza took off like a spaceship, someone's voice rang out.
The moment I lowered my right hand, your left hand
Disappeared, at once,
Into the haze.

Misunderstanding

I will be misunderstood. By you,
By the wind,
By the calendar too.

I will be misunderstood. At the breakfast table,
In front of the traffic lights,
In the subway train
That has just emerged from the long tunnel,
At last
I will brush against myself.

A sudden spell of sunlight winds itself around my thoughts
And rushes to the other side of the window.
Entwined within me, you,
The wind,
The suspect,
And the boat people at the bottom of the international section
Shimmering along the surface of the river.

You, the wind and the sunlight lost me
And within the speed of the circle line at 8 a.m.
I am fixed in a spot, a little askew.
The misunderstood, for all their lives,
Wander through another world
Tilting their heads.

Into my short dream
Someone puts his hand out
Softly.

Mannequin

One fine day
When the wind fluttered placards exceeding itself
And the broad-leaved tree transgressed itself,

I was respectful.
I imagined no obscene thoughts.
I controlled myself in every way.
So you couldn't read me.
Whenever you look at me
My silence revives.
My gaze is ready-made.

Even when fierce nights go through you
I keep a geometric pose.
Daewoo apartment stands at the end of my gaze,
I understand its standstill posture.
How boring, things that bloom and wither.
I will slowly grow old
And my last moment will be definite.

Under the placard you come towards me overflowing with yourself.
When you run out and form a long shadow,
The falling leaves that pause in the air
Cross behind you.
Alone you shake your head.
I'm sick of you.

Like Dust

I fluttered like the ears of an elephant,
You looked into the distance like the snout of a dog,
And we gently drifted through the air.

In the mirror a woman was drying her hair,
With the reflection of a man drinking *Hwalmyungsu* inside the
pharmacy,
We became our own backgrounds,
Passing endlessly by.

The world this morning was irrelevant to history and
The world last night just the world last night,
We were confused yet beautiful
Like dust
Like music.

Today someone disappeared between Seongsu and Ttukseom,
Someone leaned his head on the window like a sick Jew,
Someone hushed like a museum entrance,
And I woke up this morning like a private investigator in a
detective story.

Though veteran librarians always warn against a music analogy,
We were like pianists with our eyes on the present
To flow into the notes of the future.

Tomorrow again, I'll have curled like the neck of a giraffe.
The day after tomorrow again, you'll have become heavier like a
hippo's jaw.
After thirty years we'll have moved step by step
Like the same full dust.

Ventriloquist

1
The bygone voice
Coming back again
Like things that disappeared into drawers
Suddenly return to the drawers.

2
Suppose I come upon an alley while walking along the alley,
All I can do is to look around.
There are things that start living all of a sudden
From a place that happens all of a sudden.
The old, new world
That unrolls where the blind alley appears.

3
Perhaps there
The passage to another world opens its mouth
To almost everywhere where the lower grounds roll:
The drains beneath the walls,
The ant tunnels unseen,
Our mouths agape.

The country of the night and the calabash bottle where
Things that disappeared to another world keep surging.

4
All at once I'm drawn to look back
Like an extra in a horror film.
However, my expression attempts to bear no meaning
As much as possible.

While gazing at the place I came in holding my breath,
The contours of the thin trees changed already
And into the splinters of glass on the wall,
Yesterday's moonlight swiftly seeps.

5

Now it's time for another world to return:
A lock of hair sucked into the bathroom drain,
The natural colors faded into the black and white photos,
The ripples etched into the thin ice of the Ui Stream,
The clouds from five minutes ago.

However I keep on traveling
Whenever I look around it's there again,
The country of the night and the calabash bottle.

6

There's a time when I can feel the rotation of the earth.
The world consists of infinite alleyways.

The hieroglyphs raid you at any moment.
At last there is a day
Where another voice pours out of your interior.
Or comes back to you.

The Dirty Street

A Phone Call with Mr. Elephant

The bus driver Mr. Choi is being held at the terminal. The terminal operates the massive machines by holding on to Mr. Choi. Terminals are always in suburbs.

Yes, yes. I will get off at SK apartment. The far-off mountains of the evening are moving. On the six-lane roads, the unseen terminals are clouded.

Shit. For a while Mr. Choi stays silent and then he spits on the rush hour streets. Yet we continue our advance. The Street trees are linked firmly to the earth. The trees do not run, hop, hop, or leap off things. If we add up the distances we've moved,

Could we get back to our own place? Let's turn around and whistle. The propeller by the steering wheel pushes the air towards Mr. Choi's hair. Blind things do not stop and,

Again we think with our eyes closed. Autumn, if that autumn comes again I will ride my childhood bike. From somewhere a hand will appear and guide the rubber handlebars. The feet will propel the golden pedals. Where have the memory of our hands and feet been hidden? But I might not lose my balance. Nothing but the vanishing point in front holds me. That is my mold.

Outside the window, street trees swim up and stare at me who stays in an aquarium. That pliant expression is boring, isn't it? That's why I hate saints. He also said: Have I not chosen you, you Twelve? Yet one of you is a devil (John 6:70). I am inevitable, like watching the bottom of the eighth inning of a professional baseball game while lying on the sofa.

Next stop is SK apartment. Mr. Choi's face is on a half-size business card above the exit door. Shit, tonight as well he will spit it out with his usual look. Lard in a shot glass floating away towards the horizon,

Right, who cares? I will make a detour to avoid you. Let's not meet. That way we're connected forever. How beautiful, huh? I can't stop laughing. Bang, bang, ought to end it.

The far-off mountains follow my travels at the same latitude. They drift away brooding over the dead as they have little to say. They don't seem to get tired of that perfect balance, do they?

Through the Tollgate with the Monster

Let's draw a monster. It swings its tail, encircles, and wraps around your waist, its pointy tongue is pleasing so you burst into laughter.

Let's draw a monster crossing the Han River from this car window. It's raining, no less. It's snowing around the eyes of the monster. If it takes a step forward it might flood, and if it takes a step forward no one will look back.

Today the monster is a monster, trampling the skyscrapers, and tomorrow the monster will be a monster, its back, soft. It flaps swinging and collapses, swinging, without exception. As it opens its infinite mouth and raises its head, the music of the world fades into its mouth.

Under the monster's legs, people with umbrellas lick ice-cream. Today too, the monster is a monster, with me forever, the monster goes through the tollgate.

Trace

When traces of the ball crash against
The thin curtain of air
Inside the micro muscles of a man shooting a three-point shot

When the five fingers
Look back at themselves
For something else

When at last the air between the fingertips and the hoop
Remembers the traces of the ball
That has just passed through

When all of a sudden my murmurs of you
Teem with physical things

When my sole body looks back at
Itself in silence
Within these perfect mathematical traces

Disappearance

I was transferred to you bit by bit.
I was born outside of myself.
I recalled nothing,
Yet started fading
With unfailing precision.
While walking down the road,
Someone's memory
Lifted my hair.
The passersby watched the scene,
My feet growing away from the ground.
When my eyebrows, lips and shoulders
Were disappearing fiercely, yet calmly,
From somewhere remote
Someone suddenly
Looked back.
In the sunshine
I opened my arms as wide as possible.

We Shall Drink Chinese Alcohol Tomorrow

The streets of last night, cats infinitely sneaked into,
Hiding, running yet forever
Fading

We bought lottery tickets last year
And this year too, our life may be led
By experts

I want to block out the voices that leak out from my dreams
So as to make you generous to me

In three years I'll be happy becoming impotent by degrees
And in five years I will self-reflect after a long time

Today maybe I live like a perfect man
Yet tomorrow I'll like these kinds of things;

The staked arrow in my sleep sways from the wind
And I shall wake up tonight for no reason

Tomorrow we shall drink Chinese alcohol
And walk the streets where cats run

In the only night street of this world
All day long the windows are
Busy being transparent

We are like cats
Hiding delicately, running
Yet forever fading

Bullfighting

Between us there was a scent of something.
Between us flowers bloomed.
Between us water froze.
At least I am
Precise.

Intensely my body
Holds out.
At last I am
Extroverted. Infinitely,
I am being transferred
To you,
My sole exterior.

When a single vanishing point expands,
When I am cornered in a single vanishing point,
Is that probability?
When sunlight forms a black dot
After passing through the convex lens,

My horn has left me
And at last pierced you.
My running is afire,
In the end it will be done.
I am like a pillar of flaming ice.
Through the air thousands of footprints
Are running.

Bullfighting at Dusk

Something
Seems pervasive something
Seems decisive
The trees seem
To achieve the sky

When the steel frames of an eighteenth story high rise
And the secret between us is forgotten
And the mounds of graves grow
And the penknife from a boy's pocket blooms,

The Spanish bull looking ahead
Runs from within the television set
And nails down the geometry of the red light

There is no mistake
And the noises around him reach their peak
I want to misunderstand
Something crucially

However, the Spanish bull is already
Furious
Its horn convulsive
At some moment,

It achieves the growing reddish hue of the dusk
Standing at the flower bed of the apartment like a dead tree
The Spanish bull is
Running

Power of Stairs

Stairs bear no doubts at all
And stairs are like the music of the future.
Though you may tap-dance down the steps,
Stairs control you for only their delicacy.

As though they go on living with indifference towards others
As though they are thoughts returning precisely to their place,

Stairs lead to perfect stairs
And do not disappear all of a sudden.
You are full of stairs and now descending the stairs
And unwittingly a flight of stairs
Thus you have gained the most decent of heights
That you could ever achieve.

Suddenly you've seeped into the stairs
Like raindrops that leapt once
And vanished into another world.
Anyway, today as well we discuss
The history of stairs step by step.

Personal Life

With your own expression
You're talking to me gesticulating a bit
Café Franz mirrors you and me
And beyond the large sheet of window,
The history of a personal life flows;
It's splendid
On the street any sort of personal life can stride by
A pigeon has just made in marvelous pose,
The best descent of its life
In this city I am the only witness
I remember its pose exactly during its descent
But a child throws a very personal stone
At the unruffled pigeon and
The personal life of the pigeon topples
At last I stare at you
We are companions
Tomorrow morning the apartment will echo
With the melody that announces the recycling bin collection
Companions will fill the square and
We will cross the splendid world
And again if a splendid afternoon comes
We will march honorably into the Changrim Gimbab bistro
Sweeping the glass doors open, in tracksuits, in slippers,
Right at the moment
When the pigeon catches a glimpse of me through the window,
Taking off again for the best descent of its life

Addiction

This afternoon I walk again the street of yesterday. The sunset beyond the Hyundai department store. It's almost an addiction. But yesterday I also walked along the distant seashore of the sunset.

Now, tired of three-dimensions. I mean, depth. Please unfold and slip me in between the leaves of a book. A silent plane. Someday you will open an old book I've marked and. Walk the depthless seashore again.

The sea, a sheer plane. When I draw a long line with a pencil from you, who stare out at the sea, something reaches out to a dot somewhere. Say that dot is an island. And you sleep without dreams on the island. You fold me into a paper airplane and a paper boat, and a thin paper crane.

Thus everything has gone amiss. With things, emptied-interior like a silent plane. The sunset beyond the Hyundai department store, like a man sinking into a swamp step by step. A paper airplane has just taken off from the rooftop of the department store, where its gloomy edges are poised against the sunset.

Matters

Stones are irrelevant to me
Signboards are irrelevant to me
I fall into a subtle silence

As a single matter, if you bloom in front of me
I will gaze back at you
As if praying

When the long-sodden people between us
Bloom and wither,
As though stroking stones
As though staring at signboards,

Steadily,
I will soak into you,
Into your doubtful looks

Outside the office window
A placard flutters;
"Believe in the Lord Jesus, and
You will be saved — you and your household."

After sitting absently for a while,
I find my dead friend's number
And pick up the receiver

A Geometrical Composition

Again and again he reverts to:
A single dot. Robinson Crusoe's raft breaking desperately through
the horizon. The last target which a member of the national
archery team aims at. The eyes of a kingfisher
Slicing through the water below while making its delicate descent.

But regardless of his gaze at the cable television programs,
At dawn in the sofa, he splits again into infinite targets.
His stomach full of all kinds of food. His blood following irregular
circulation cycles.
The geometry of his hair and toenails,
Though unseen,
Strains out in all directions

The vanishing points in the air that converge on his body
Become the core of gravity that acts on his fall
From the fifteenth floor,
Or a single dot that traps him.
Let the stomach, toenails, blood,
And hair hear the whistle.

When I turn and look outside the window,
A lost dog indifferently draws
A diagonal line on the plane of the crossroad at dawn.
The 100 km/h machines
Brush against the edges of his ears.
The sun at six o'clock in the morning
Has paused in the image of verticality
Breaking the infinite lines of steel.

Run, Bus, Run

When the number 7 bus that I'm on shakes
I am only the number 7 bus. Up three centimeters in the air
I sense every part of myself.
I don't remember, don't think, most of all,
Don't allow any mistakes.

At that moment flowers burst into bloom in one direction
And a boy nods with a different expression
And the smoke in the sky turns into non-smoke.

At last when unfamiliar winds rock the road in harmony
    with the flowers
And the ferocious circulation of the boy's blood removes him,
The smoke in the sky has erased itself in silence
By forming fine paths in the air.

I wonder which thoughts have seized me so far;
At the terminal for number 7,
I'm staring vaguely at the children run, whooshing their way home.

Shaking my head boldly
I'll walk on the road where flowers endlessly bloom,
After all this afternoon is for not remembering,
Not thinking,
Not allowing any mistakes,
At the crossroad a few buses
Are speeding fiercely.

Knife

Things seen in holding a knife:
Tranquil spaces between the bones that
This lucent edge will pass through.

In the end we will be lonely.
We will know that when letting something else in.
The yellow tape on the first floor steps of Miseong tenement
Thrusting darkness like a barricade;
DO NOT CROSS, Gangbuk Police Station.

The midnight apartment's playground, it's enough to feel dizzy.
The stars revolve feebly.
I want to meet a phantom in an ambush somewhere.
Or perhaps my dead mother.

My targets are merely
Night clouds lowering their altitude.
Once I stabbed those clouds.
As well as the dusk or the sea.
What an interior, letting everything in.

The man stabbed the woman from Miseong tenement
Very meticulously.
From the inside of the knife the clouds,
The dusk and the sea do not sway.
I raise it and stare at the woman's last look
Mirrored in the blade.

The stars facing the yellow tape of Miseong tenement,
Pass through the spaces, somehow
Gloomy and tranquil.

Today as well the Night

The humans of the night began to move.

We said no words like wicked monsters.
We kept going forward
Like the slow movements of creatures with eight feet,
Not imagining beyond the glimmers of the night sky.

Foul rain falls.
I'm not curious of your blood type
And as time goes by, tomorrow,
The day after tomorrow,
And the roadkilled cat last night
Grow distant.

We never spoke negatively.
No one ran short of music.
We were absorbed in ourselves
As if waiting for a call from some petty fate.

Now I have become pitch black like the night itself
And you have become truly honest.
Though that has been our long-lived misfortune.

Shouldn't think too much.
At last, we are old and wise like cats on the road.
You have no desire to breed
And I have another world.

We fell asleep as if being reminded of it.
We will wake as wicked monsters at last.
As the humans of the night,
Delightful and ordinary,
As the humans of the night.

Suspect

#1 Moran Motel at dawn
Removal. I am a removal man.

#2 Bathroom
The mirror absorbs me whenever I brush my teeth. In those moments I am a man captured only by my teeth. I'm persistent to remove the traces of yesterday with the simple look in the mirror that obeys the order.

#3 A meal with you at a Chinese restaurant
It's not for an alibi that I meet you, but as I meet you I disappear in silence. You, before me, have no doubt about me as ever. That is a kind of habit. My whereabouts are turned into vague rumors in *The Daily Sports, National Geographic* and *YTN*—sometimes with cigarette smoke.

#4 Hideout
Should buy cigarettes and a newspaper. Make sure to observe the interior of habits. Where I can perfectly hide myself.

#5 LG 25
To prove that nobody doubts me, I observe the woman from the convenience store, and the man at the newsstand. There comes a time when those looks remove me forever. Then I leave the convenience store and the newsstand. Though the removed things are still on the hunt for me, I turn around and step into the alley.

#6 Naebalsan-dong
Day and night transform each other to destroy evidence. Yet everything is suspicious. My trace is relative. Where are you now?

#7 What comes across the dusk
Thus there is a moment of strange sympathy; that right now someone else is staring at the dusk that I am staring at now.
I'm embarrassed. I am irrelevant to you who come across to me through the dusk. The dusk is a trivial coincidence as usual.

#8 Samsung Pavv
In the end I am a stone on the roadside. You will discover me by degrees; I'll get kicked by chance and reveal my whole small story before you. On the Samsung Pavv displayed in the show window, the *National Geographic* takes a close-up of the horn of a water buffalo, the sun on the grassland moves visibly or invisibly, against the horn.

#9 Moran Motel at midnight
Silence. What comes back again.
Silence.

Interview with an Alien

I smile as if hearing something humorous
That is my way
For instance, I am a different kind than dog or cat

When veiled things are near me
I just stare into space,
Makeshifts are always available

You will understand me by degrees
The speed at which I speak is not the speed but
My metamorphosis,
I am involved with myself, so from me and to me,
I go on to the end

Let us love addicts
They are easily careless
About the world outside
Though I'm remade every second,
I voice my trust in you, uncertain,
And laugh bashfully
Someday for the far-off mountains,
For the night sky,
And for the galaxy beyond,
I'd like to let loose one legendary joke
So as to make the cats
And the dogs
And the earthlings of the world all smile together

We are all sharp and dark
Like the addict's lonely night

For the far-off mountains and you
I am being transformed at heart
Carefully
Carefully

Your Active Boundary

You were a bed,
Wide open
Like a curtain,
And turned into the laughter of a fatalist
And chopped in two
Like a mackerel on a cutting board

When the afternoon came you were
Displayed among the goods of Shinsegae Department Store
And became another world,
Gone but once close to coming out as words
You stuck between the teeth
Rotting unnoticed

After falling down from the twelfth floor
You went back up via the elevator
And turned into the dark night
So cried out the dim, old love
You cried out
And after washing your face
You appeared on the home shopping channel
And at once, turned into the bed again

Today's Weather

From Geneva to Moscow
And from Moscow to Seoul
We are linked by sleep.
We are connected by absent bodies. At last
Countless fingers point at nothing.
In my sleep
I have no responsibility towards you.

All love fades into a healthy routine.
How can we bear it?
But today I have a dinner engagement.
Under the rays of the sunset
A man flops down by the crosswalk at Jongno sam-ga
And nods off.

Simultaneously we recall
The world made of quadrilaterals like an elevator.
Something descends within us.
We may meet in our worn out sleep,
Today's weather, from Seoul to Geneva
And from Geneva to Moscow,
Has been stable.

From this morning to the next tomorrow
Please forget me.
Let's welcome the splendid morning with handstands.
Handstands are lonesome.
You look upside down and
Into today's weather, I'm
Descending forever.

My Gloomy Modern Boy

"Alleys," as thus pronounced repeatedly, the alleys start disappearing slowly. By the alleys, from the alleys, through the alleys, at the alleys... But there are alleys outside the window. I open the fridge and take out the milk. Tomorrow is Election Day. The sell-by date on the carton has expired.

However, the music is a ballad. Once I read a piece, "Baek Seok Is A Modern Boy," written by poet Oh Jang-hwan. I walk towards Kookmin Bank to check my part-time pay. Tomorrow is Election Day. Baek Seok is a modern boy.

Perhaps I am still overloaded. Rollerblades vanish blindly ahead. Don't look behind. Otherwise I'll turn into a pillar of salt. By the alleys, as the alleys, with the alleys, at last the alleys... I walk.

I recognize him from a distance, the boss of the computer repair shop, Mr. Kim, once a revolutionary, and perhaps still one. I take another alley and keep walking. By the alleys, through the alleys, with the alleys, at last the alleys...

Once he called me a romantic animal, but that night he left for the East Sea, without me. The sandstorm from the apartment construction site sweeps through the alleys. A close up of the daily paid worker's helmet says, 'Safety First'. Baek Seok is not a modern boy.

No record of part-time pay in the bankbook. Things rise up gradually when I narrow my eyes. For instance from the alleys, with the alleys, at the alleys, of the alleys... A ballad, the music that played in the Doremi Record store.

Tomorrow is Election Day. A few magpies fly away after resting on the signboard for Kookmin Bank. The waves of the East Sea surge in a sparse and definite posture, from the sky somewhere far away towards the alleys, from the alleys, of the alleys, through the alleys I walk.

Spread

He evaporated
In a flash.
Though no one turned their heads
When he was talking with you
His wrists were gone.
While watching his arms disappear,
You talked about the penalty shootout, Korea vs. Japan.

His legs erased and his waist,
His shoulders,
Eliminated.
As his lips vanished
Calmly you reached
The climax of the conversation.
He left his form casually
As outside the window a dry snow fell.

His percolation on you;
During the meal,
At the bank,
In the immersion of sex,
And from the persistent impulse to murder,

You recognize it.
You felt a gust of tears
In the business section of the morning newspaper,
From the voice on the receiver,
And in yourself.
You thought of him, his infinite spread.
As he made you out,
He rapped your shoulder
And passed on by.

The Secrets of Birds

Between us there was a secret.
I went silent.
The marching passersby stuffed tight with
Trivial secrets, we are about to burst
In a second.
I may remove my face
And turn into another
That remembers the old one
Yet the bird's low flight
Is hidden forever
Between the stars unseen.
A man who counts change at the street stand
Might forget the dead woman for a while
And that moment a one-year-old tree's roots
Might slowly reach out to her darkness
A garbage truck drifts through the city
I support the Democratic Labor Party,
And the earth rotates on and on.
Satellites cross over my head.
Today's weather is fine.
And perhaps tomorrow's too.